Praise For Born Creative

Harry Hoover has produced a book well worth the read if you are looking for tools to improve your personal or group's creative process. He correctly insists that if we are to expand our inventive horizons, we must first believe in ourselves and in our own potential for creativity. His writing style is practical, thankfully lacking in the kind of psycho-babble often associated with other books on the subject. Hoover's straight forward ideas combined with inspiring illustrations, come from a writer who has obviously mastered personal creativity through years of thinking and then creating. I wholeheartedly recommend the book. As the title suggests, free your mind – free yourself.

— Kenneth Mills, Ph.D., Counseling Psychologist, Cognitive Behavioral Therapist

―――――――――

Quick, deceptively simple ways to boost your creativity. I've taught classes and offered workshops for years on developing the creative process — and this book offers helpful techniques in an effective, do-it-yourself format. You have the potential to be creative — we all do. The only question is whether you've developed your ability. Here are plenty of exercises, supported by solid research, to help you make the most of your creative ability. Being able to spot issues, solve problems, encourage others — all those are competitive advantages in any setting. This book offers practical application rather than mere theory — something you can pick up and start using.

— Cathy Pickens, Author of the Avery Andrews Southern mystery series, former college business professor, and Queens University provost

—————————

What a great resource to help jumpstart anyone's creativity! First Harry Hoover debunks the idea that only some people are born creative. He makes the case that we all are and then provides a toolbox full of ideas to spur us on. A fun quick read, this book is one I will refer to often. I loved his take on brainstorming. As someone who has sat through far too many brainstorming sessions, I absolutely agree that it's an exercise for one. Another approach he suggests, which was new to me, is having someone write three ideas on paper and passing it on to the next person to do the same. At the end, a robust list of ideas is ready for discussion, without the inevitable judgment that creeps in during brainstorming sessions. The book is full of different ways to look at any situation. So simple, yet brilliant. I can't wait to put his ideas into practice.

— Marcia Merrill, Owner of marketing/PR firm, Red Rover Communications

Born Creative: Free Your Mind, Free Yourself

HARRY HOOVER

Contents

"Everyone is born creative; everyone is given a box of crayons in kindergarten. Then when you hit puberty they take the crayons away and replace them with dry, uninspiring books on algebra, history, etc. Being suddenly hit years later with the 'creative bug' is just a wee voice telling you, 'I'd like my crayons back, please'." – Hugh MacLeod

Humans are innately creative: all humans, including you.

I take my definition of creativity from Author Robert E. Franken, who said, "creativity is the tendency to generate or recognize ideas, alternatives or possibilities that may be useful in solving problems, communicating with others, as well as entertaining ourselves and others."

You'll notice that definition never mentions artistic ability. People often tell me they are not creative and then go on to tell me how they can't draw or paint. Artistic ability is a creative talent, but creativity is more than the ability to wield a paintbrush – so much more.

"Everyone is a genius. But if you judge a fish by its ability to climb a tree, it will live its whole life believing it is stupid," – Albert Einstein

This book is about the full range of creativity: your human inheritance. It will provide you with the information and motivation you need to unlock your innate creative abilities. And, I believe, it will set you on a path toward more personal freedom.

Your innate creativity can help you design the life you

desire. Once you master the ability to let your ideas flow at will, you'll realize that there is nothing that can hold you back. The mind is like a muscle and has to be exercised to improve. And you'll get plenty of exercise via this book.

There is only one thing that I will ask of you as you read this: believe you are creative. This belief, or removal of self-doubt, is a consistent theme in the book. *Born Creative* will help you get there. If you are of that mindset already, our work is more than half done. If you don't believe that you are creative, I hope to convince you that you are wrong, so that you can free your mind, and then free yourself.

Let's get started turning you into an idea machine.

Harry Hoover

CHAPTER 1

You and Your Brain

Since humans swung naked out of the trees onto the Serengeti plains, we have been creative. We had to be. Look at us. Scrawny and hairless surrounded by big cats and other predators. If we had not used those big brains, cockroaches would probably be at the top of today's food chain.

We figured out how to form communities to provide safety for ourselves, developed weapons for self-defense, as well as to acquire the protein necessary to fuel our bodies and our big brains. Did you know that our brains utilize about 20 percent of our energy? Early man – drained from all that thinking – was probably really happy when he discovered how to generate fire that would keep him warm and help cook his food.

Shortly after man harnessed fire and developed more of a sense of community – between 40,000 and 60,000 years ago – he started developing better weapons, drawing on the cave walls, and probably spinning yarns for entertainment.

The early Egyptians had some rudimentary technical

knowledge of the brain. We have evidence that they performed cranial surgery.

We've continued throughout human history to grapple with the question: how does the brain work?

Science tells us that 95 percent of what we know about the brain, we have learned in the last 30 years or so. Your beliefs about creativity were probably shaped by faulty information. For instance, many believe that only special, talented people are creative – and you have to be born that way.

Wrong.

The notion that geniuses such as Shakespeare, Picasso and Mozart were anymore `gifted' than you is a myth, according to a study at Exeter University. Researchers examined outstanding performances in the arts, mathematics and sports, to find out if "the widespread belief that to reach high levels of ability a person must possess an innate potential called talent."

This particular study concludes that "talent" is determined by five key elements:

1. **Opportunities**
2. **Encouragement**
3. **Training**
4. **Motivation**
5. **Practice** (this one, most of all)

The research also indicates that few showed early signs of promise prior to parental encouragement, and no one reached high levels of achievement in their field without devoting thousands of hours of serious training. Consider Mozart who trained for 16 years before he produced an acknowledged masterwork.

All of this is interesting and enlightening but doesn't necessarily get to the root of the issue of creativity. I think there is one element even more important than the five mentioned above. Let me tell you a true story to illustrate what I think is the prime factor in creativity.

A New York publisher was concerned about the lack of creativity among his editorial and marketing staff. He hired psychologists to try to determine what differentiated the creative employees from the others. After a year of study, the psychologists discovered that there was only one difference between creative and non-creative employees: belief in their creativity.

Creative employees believed they were creative, and the non-creative ones believed they were not.

As Henry Ford purportedly said, "Whether you think you can or think you can't, you are right."

A Harvard Business Review (HBR) study of its database of 6,000 professionals who have taken the Innovator's DNA assessment further supports the supposition that you must believe in your creativity to make it so.

The study found that those who agree with the survey statement "I am creative" consistently create new businesses, products, services and processes that no one has done before. Because they see themselves as creative, they are. HBR data further suggests that if you change your "I'm not creative" mindset, you too, can become more consistently creative. HBR has developed a simple, five question test to help you determine your creative mindset.

Answer these questions with a Yes or a No:

Associational thinking: I creatively solve challenging problems by drawing on diverse ideas or knowledge.

Questioning: I often ask questions that challenge others' fundamental assumptions.

Observing: I get innovative ideas by directly observing how people interact with products and services.

Idea Networking: I regularly talk with a diverse set of people (e.g., from different functions, industries, geographies) to find and refine new business ideas.

Experimenting: I frequently experiment to create new ways of doing things.

According to HBR, if you answered no to three or more of the questions you are most likely in the "I'm not creative" mindset. But you can change.

As cartoonist Hugh MacLeod says, "Everyone is born creative; everyone is given a box of crayons in kindergarten. Then when you hit puberty they take the crayons away and replace them with dry, uninspiring books on algebra, history, etc. Being suddenly hit years later with the 'creative bug' is just a wee voice telling you, "I'd like my crayons back, please."

Let's get out our crayons – and our belief in our creativity – shall we?

Did You Know?

- Research shows that everyone has creative abilities. The more training you have and the more diverse the training, the greater is your potential for creative output.

- Additionally, it has been shown that in creativity quantity equals quality. In fact, the longer the list of ideas, the higher the quality of the final solution. Typically, the highest quality ideas appear at the end of the list.

- The average adult thinks of three to six alternatives for any given situation. The average child thinks of 60.

- A study at Rhode Island College showed that a moderate amount of exercise improves creativity.

- Creativity is an individual process. Traditional brainstorming has been proven ineffective because of fear of social disapproval.

- Groups are best for idea selection and evaluation rather than idea generation.

CHAPTER 2

The Big Creativity Roadblock

Self-Doubt & How To Beat It

I have always considered myself creative. But sometimes even creative folks get stuck. In 1999, I picked up a book that changed the way I think – and subsequently – changed my life for the better.

I'm a fan of Leonardo da Vinci, so when I saw Michael Gelb's book, *How To Think Like Leonardo da Vinci*, I bought it. It contains exercises to help you incorporate da Vinci's principles of creativity into your life.

The one thing that had the most profound impact on me was Gelb's power question: what one thing could I stop doing, start doing or do differently today that would most improve the quality of my life? My answer: stop commuting two hours per day for work. My children were moving into middle and high school and I didn't want to turn around one day to find them to be strangers.

Because as Entrepreneur David Norris has said, "How

you spend your time is more important than how you spend your money. Money mistakes can be corrected, but time is gone forever."

Now, once you answer your power question, you must develop a plan to achieve it. I figured that if you work from home, no driving is involved. You can spend more time with your family and actually have more productive work time as well. I believed I could make it happen. It took several months of thinking, planning, and believing but I was able to successfully launch my first company in 2001. There were fits and starts along the way, but my company grew and evolved into the company that I formed in 2007 with my business partner, Brant Waldeck, My Creative Team.

You, too, are creative and can take charge of your life the way I did. I guarantee it. All you have to do is believe me. Is that too much to ask?

CHAPTER 3

The "I Am" List

Everyone has an inner negative voice, telling them they are no good, or that they can't do something.

We've all had that teacher who because we were left-handed and had poor handwriting told us we couldn't draw either. Oh, maybe that was just me.

Anyway, with this exercise, we are going to override that negative voice with some positive affirmation.

Right now, get a pen or pencil and make a list using 31 blanks as shown below. Begin with the #2 spot and make a list of 30 things you do well. I don't care what they are. Could be that you can grill a superb steak, select a great bottle of wine, or calm a crying infant. Doesn't matter – just make the list.

List done? OK, at the top of the list add your #1 item: **I am really creative**.

Put the list somewhere you will see it every evening, and before you go to bed, read it to yourself for the next 10 days. Read it every morning when you get up, too.

The brain knows you are trying to "fool" it but falls for it every time.

I Am:

1. _____
   _____

2. _____
   _____

3. _____
   _____

4. _____
   _____

5. _____
   _____

6. _____
   _____

7. _____
   _____

8. _____
   _____

9. _____
   _____

10. _____
    _____

11. _____
    _____

12. _____
    _____

13. _____
    _____

14. _____
    _____

15. _____
    _____

16. _____
    _____

17. _____
    _____

18. _____
    _____

19. _____
    _____

20. _____
    _____

21. _____
    _____

22. _____
    _____

23. _____
    _____

24. _____
    _____

25. _____
    _____

26. _____

27. _____

28. _____

29. _____

30. _____

31. _____

CHAPTER 4

A Fish Tale

Let me tell you a true, but sad, fish story. Scientists in New England were studying this big fish living in a large tank. He had everything a fish could want. At feeding time the scientists would drop minnows into the fish's tank. He would eat them. This required no effort on his part. Life was good, or so he thought at the time.

One day at feeding time, the big fish found that his minnows were encased in glass tubes. He could see the minnows swimming inside the tubes but could not eat them no matter how hard he tried. And he tried everything: slamming the glass tubes against the side of the tank, swatting it with his tail. Nothing worked. But the big fish learned through his repeated efforts that he could not get to the fish. He gave up.

Next, the scientists pulled all the small fish and their tubes out of the tank, removed them from the tubes and dropped them back in right beside the big fish, who by this time was starving. Here comes the sad part. The big fish, surrounded by this bounty, starved to death.

He no longer believed he could eat the fish, so he no longer tried.

Don't be the big fish.

You are creative. Believe it and make it so.

CHAPTER 5

How To Brainstorm

I am a fan of individual brainstorming. This can be a good way for you to think through a problem. There is only one rule to follow – initially, there are no bad ideas. Just write down everything that occurs to you and come back later to sort out the wheat from the chaff.

However, I think group brainstorming is typically a waste of time. Brainstorming doesn't work – at least it doesn't work the way that most people approach it in the corporate world. They try to generate ideas and allow criticism of those ideas at the same time. This makes participants shut down. People are afraid to voice ideas that may get them ridiculed. So, you need to segregate idea generation from the winnowing process. Even with rules in place, group brainstorming is problematic. If you can't change your organizational belief that brainstorming is a waste of time, my top 7 tips will help you mount a successful brainstorming session.

1. Proper Preparation. Make sure you have a clear idea of the session's purpose. Too often, brainstorming sessions get off target because a clear agenda has not been outlined. Remember, creativity is best facilitated if participants are provided with some parameters ahead of time.

2. Select a facilitator for the session. An outsider, who has nothing to gain or lose from the results, is best. Next, pick a manageable size group of six to nine people from varied backgrounds, age and job responsibilities. Consider an off-site location to help make the point that you are not looking for the usual thinking that happens at your place of business.

3. Generate, Don't Denigrate. I saw this phrase "Generate, Don't Denigrate" in an article years ago and it has stuck with me because it is so important to the process. This is where most brainstorming goes wrong. Your mission is to generate ideas without commenting, criticizing, or offering opinions. You don't want to slow down the process or make participants skittish about sharing their ideas. Just crank out the ideas, then record them somewhere so you can go back later to discuss, combine, or weed out. You are going for quantity. This is the best way to get great ideas. Typically, when adults are asked for ideas, they come up with 6 – 8 on the subject. Children will generate 50 or more. Your job is to think like a kid.

4. Suspend judgment. No criticizing or discussing an idea. As people express ideas, they are simply recorded. This can be done on post-its, lap-tops or flip charts but don't find fault or make comments, as this slows the process of idea flow. A good way to avoid criticism is to have participants write ideas down and hand them to the facilitator. This ensures that no one knows who came up with the idea.

5. Go for quantity. Quantity leads to quality in brainstorms so don't stop until you have a large number of ideas – typically 60 to 100 or more.

6. Go beyond reason. Wild ideas are useful because they challenge boundaries and provoke other fresh ideas. It is easier to tame a wild idea than to inject something radical into a bland one

7. Piggyback. When one person suggests a creative concept others should chip in with extensions, developments and specific ways to make it happen. Piggyback on each other's notions.

Bonus Tip. My bonus tip helps totally remove the fear of public ridicule from the equation. Assemble a group. Have each person write down three ideas on a piece of paper and pass it to the person to their right. That person reads the ideas and adds three more ideas triggered by the previous ideas. This continues until it gets back to the beginning and all the ideas are shared with the group.

MORE BRAINSTORMING TIPS

- Encourage participants to give thought to the problem prior to the session.

- Set a time limit.

- Capture everything in writing.

- Let one word or thought suggest another.

- Think positive.

- Exclude negatives.

- Imagine no budget restraints, no one to say, "That won't work."

- Stuck? Move on. Come back later.

- Don't sweat the details.

CHAPTER 6

Creativity Exercises

Creativity often needs a little nudge. Sometimes, it can be a subtle shift in thinking, sometimes it takes an earthquake to boost the brain. Luckily, other creative folks have come before us and given us some guidance on the matter. Let's take a look at some of these creativity exercises to boost our little gray cells.

Dictionary Excursion

Let's head to the dictionary for a creativity boost. Here's what I want you to do:

You're going to select six words from a dictionary and use them to write a story of less than 250 words. You will select your six words from your dictionary on:

- page 52, 11th word down write word here:

  _____

- page 111, 2nd word down write word here:

  _____

- page 144, 1st word down write word here:

  _____

- page 199, 9th word down write word here:

  _____

- page 225, 12th word down write word here:

  _____

- page 243, 6th word down write word here:

  _____

Now, that you have your six words, open the dictionary at random, close your eyes, and select a word. That word will provide the subject of your story.

Write your story subject word here: _____

Use the first three words in your opening paragraph. The last three words may be sprinkled throughout the story. Now, start writing.

Change The Question

Sometimes just by changing a word or two in a question, you can come up with radically different solutions to problems.

Centuries ago a plague spread across Europe which was almost always fatal. In one town, a person thought to be dead was buried alive. The townspeople wanted to make sure this didn't happen again. One group proposed putting food and water in every casket and an air hole up to the surface. Their question: "what if we bury someone alive?" Another group suggested placing a 12-inch spike in the coffin lid and aligning it with the victim's heart. Their question: "how do we make sure everyone we bury is dead?"

Do you have a current problem in which changing the question might help?

Random Input

A random piece of information often can boost your problem-solving process into hyperdrive. Once you have your question or problem clearly stated, open up a dictionary or a thesaurus to any page and select a word. Now, think about how this random item applies to your problem. There is some connection and your job is to find it.

Urban Photo Adventure

Creativity happens when you let it, not when you try to force it. That's why you get your best ideas when running or showering. Your mind is typically in neutral in those situations and ideas seem to occur spontaneously. So, what can you do to put your mind in neutral and spark some creativity?

You can go on an urban photo adventure. Instead of just seeing your city, observe it. Look at things you've passed by hundreds of times but in a different way.

It's easy to find beauty in a natural setting, but not as

easy in a gritty urban environment. You need to look at things differently to find the hidden beauty in the man-made inner city. What kinds of urban items can you find that have their own type of beauty?

Look closely at some of the photos I've taken. Sometimes beauty is in the tiny detail, as in the photo above. Or, sometimes it is in the shadows, as in the following photograph.

Often, you'll find unique colors in interesting juxtaposition. Is nature taking over your urban environment? There are lots of lines and angles in the city, as in this New York City wharf photo. Can you use them to your advantage photographically?

Here are a few more suggestions to guide your photo excursion.

Leading lines. When you look at a photo, your eye naturally follows lines. I've used this element of composition in this fountain photo.

Notice how your eye is naturally drawn to the jets of water heading toward the central fountain.

Framing. The world is full of elements you can use to frame a photo. Notice in the fountain photo how I have used the trees and the round concrete elements to help frame the subject. In the urban environment, you might find archways, doors, and windows that can be used to frame your photo.

Rule of thirds. Imagine that your photo is divided into nine sections – three across and three down. Instead of centering your subject, try positioning it along the intersection of these thirds. In the fountain photo, I have captured the jets of water overlapping at these points in the photo.

Symmetry & Patterns. We find symmetry and patterns all around us. Some natural. Some man-made. The jets of water in the fountain photo take advantage of symmetry. Look at window placement while on your urban photo adventure. Look at chain link fences. Can you use the pattern in a fence as an element of composition in your photo?

Now, get out your camera or smartphone and start your urban photo adventure.

The Reframing Matrix

Michael Morgan developed this tool in his 1993 book, *Creating Workforce Innovation*. If you are faced with a business-related problem, this is a good approach. Draw a box on a piece of paper and then divide it into quadrants. At the center of the paper where the lines intersect, draw a smaller box. Inside this smaller box, write the problem you want to explore. Each of the larger boxes provides space for you to look at the problem from four perspectives. I like to use the four professions approach. In one box, I might look at the problem as if I were an engineer. In the other boxes, I may use the perspective of a doctor, a grocer, and a musician. You also can use the 4Ps approach, filling in the big boxes with:

- Product perspective – What problems exist with the product/service? Does it meet customer needs? How is our price compared to competitors? Could we add or subtract something to improve the product?

- Planning perspective – How could we improve

our business or marketing plan? Is our strategy on point? Could our tactics be off the mark?

- <u>Potential perspective</u> – What can we do to increase sales to existing customers or new customers? How would we handle a flood of new customers? If we begin producing at higher volumes, how does this affect us?

- <u>People perspective</u> – What do our customers think of our product/service? How do our salespeople and distributors feel about the product?

How can you use the matrix in your world?

Circle Up

Using only circles, draw as many different things as you can in one minute. Go!

The Mindmap

Get a large piece of paper and a marker. Now, in the center of the paper write down a topic you want to explore. It can be anything from "how can I turn a hobby into a business" to "what elements make for a great party?" Circle the topic and then think about what you can add to the list. As you add items, draw lines between thoughts that seem to connect. Draw boxes around what seem to be key thoughts. At first, you will come up with cliches but keep pushing. Soon, you will start to develop wilder and more unpredictable ideas. I often find it helpful to develop the primary mindmap and then come a few days later to explore some thoughts that I found intriguing.

Six-Word Story

Write a story using only six words. It's not easy but when done well, can really evoke an emotional response. For instance: *For sale: baby shoes, never worn.* Now, that gets you thinking, doesn't it?

CHAPTER 7

SCAMMPERR For Creativity

Everything new is a modification of something existing, according to Michael Michalko, developer of a brainstorming tool called *Thinkpak*. I can't disagree with his assessment. *Thinkpak* uses the mnemonic device – **SCAMMPERR** to help you look at things in a different way. So, when creating a new product, service, idea, or process, you can use this device to help.

SCAMMPERR stands for:
S – Substitute something
C – Combine it with something else
A – Adapt something to it
M – Magnify or add to it
M – Modify it
P – Put it to some other uses

E – Eliminate something
R – Rearrange it
R – Reverse it

Substitute

Let's say you are a manufacturer of battery-powered products but want to eliminate the need for disposable batteries. What could you do? A small solar cell might give you enough power if it is a product primarily used in daylight, or the solar cell could power up a rechargeable battery. Alternatively, you could substitute a hand-cranked generator for the batteries.

A company thinks its spectacles are too heavy. What might they substitute to take weight out of their product? Would another material help? Perhaps they could substitute plastic for glass in the lenses. Or, use a lighter metal like titanium for the frames. Is there another approach? Contact lenses would really take the weight out.

Some of the key questions you can ask using the substitute approach include:

What can be substituted? Who can be substituted? What other part can be substituted? What other process would work better? What other place would work better?

What other perspective could be substituted? For

example, how would Leonardo da Vinci view the problem?

What problems do you have that could be solved with substitution?

Combine It

Creativity in new products and services often comes from combining things that may have been previously unrelated. Gutenberg's printing press, for example, combined a wine press and a coin punch. Once upon a time, you went to the grocery store, the gas station, and a fast-food restaurant. Then, someone had the idea that you could combine those into a single location. Or, there is the optical lens company that thought to combine their technology that darkens as the light gets brighter with window glass.

When thinking through a problem and considering how to combine disparate elements, here are some questions to ask:

– What ideas, processes, or parts can be combined?

– What purposes or objectives can be combined?

– Can I combine or merge it with other objects, processes or ideas?

– What can be combined to maximize the number of uses?

– How could you combine talent and resources to create a new approach to this product?

– What materials could be combined?

Adapt

In order to be an original thinker, you must first know about the ideas of others. Sometimes you can pick up an idea from one arena and adapt it to work in another. So, you start trying to adapt by first asking:

– What have others done?

– How would a scientist, preacher, artist, criminal or professional athlete approach this problem?

– Can I adapt something from nature?

– How would a dinosaur, a bird or an insect handle this?

– Are there specific objects in nature for which there is an analogy? For instance, my topic is like an avalanche because...

In 1956 a pair of brothers who sold water pumps for farm use took their knowledge of pumps to design a special whirlpool bath to treat their cousin's arthritis. The product didn't take off until they incorporated the whirlpool action into luxury bathtubs. You might have heard of the brothers Jacuzzi.

Magnify

The first question is what if we made it larger? In the 1920s a man named George Cullen took a plan for a huge grocery store to company officials at Kroger. They pooh-poohed the idea and Cullen opened America's first supermarket. Walmart and Target took that idea and magnified it even further.

How about taking it from large to gigantic? PR practitioners have been doing this for years to get publicity. They've promoted everything from the world's largest cheese to the world's largest donut. Check the Guinness Book of World's Records if you don't believe that gigantic things are effective.

What can be added? I'm glad you asked. Cracker Jacks added a prize. Proctor & Gamble added air to make Ivory Soap float. Can you add something to your offering that makes it stand out?

A few other questions can help us magnify our offerings:

What can be extended?

Can it be made longer, taller, higher, fatter?

Are there extra features that can be added?

How can we add more value?

Modify

NASCAR was born when someone decided to modify an automobile right off the dealer's lot to get more speed from it. A lot of creative ideas are the result of modification.

Speaking of automobiles, one of the biggest turnarounds in automotive history was the result of modification. The Ford Motor Company once controlled 60 percent of the automotive market, selling only black cars. GM began thinking about modification and came up with the mission to develop "a car with every shape and color for every purse and purpose." By modifying cars to meet the market's needs, GM took the market share lead.

How can you use modification to solve a problem? Start by asking questions.

What can be modified? How can it be changed for the better?

Can you change its meaning, purpose, use, dimensions, process, or character?

How about color, sound, odor, form, or function? Could you change its name?

Can you think of three small changes that could be made immediately?

Can you change the way you look at the subject? Are you able to restate the problem in five different ways?

We have started shooting some testimonial videos with iPhones. You can see one here: https://www.youtube.com/watch?v=TWwCZ-vox3M

It made subjects less nervous to have a phone pointed at them than to have a video crew looming over them. And it gave a more authentic feel to the videos.

Put It To Some Other Use

Humans have been doing it for years: taking one thing and putting it to another use. George Washington Carver, for instance, took the lowly peanut and re-purposed it into 300 other products. Consider 3M, which was trying to develop an adhesive that was not very sticky for use on bulletin boards. That never caught on, but a 3M chemist had the insight to use it on notepaper and Post-Its were born.

What else could you do with your products and services? To answer this question, you must first turn off preconceived notions and look at the problem afresh, as a 12-year-old might.

Could it do more things, as does the Swiss Army Knife? Can you modify it some way to fit a new use?

Can you find other functions, purposes, or relationships? Could you spin it off into something new?

Is anything being wasted in your process? Could that be put to some use?

One company received paper that was too thick for the toilet paper it manufactured and they didn't want to waste it. They asked, "what else can we do with this?" And the paper towel was born. Goodyear Tire developed a pollution-free furnace that burns discarded tires, converting them to energy.

How could your product or service be used in a different market, country, or field?

What's the most unusual, impractical, or silliest new use you can think of?

Eliminate

Originally, the doughnut had no hole. As legend would have it, a small boy noticed that the center of his mother's donuts wasn't completely done so he poked it out with a fork. Sometimes, as the doughnut illustrates, eliminating something makes for a more successful product.

Are there things you can eliminate from your product or service that strips it down to its essence? For instance, take away the armament from a tank and you have a tractor. The founder of Toyota took a hint from American grocery stores. He noticed that they didn't store perishables on site. Instead, the grocery pushed the storage and delivery back onto vendors. This so-called "just-in-time" concept cut Toyota's costs drastically.

How can we divide it, split it, or cut back on it to improve it? The potato chip was born when a chef was tired of a diner sending deep-fried potato slices back to the kitchen saying they were too thick. The chef, in a pique, cut them wafer-thin, fried them, and took them out. They were a hit, and the rest is history.

Here are some other questions to ask in your attempt to "eliminate" creatively:

- What if this were smaller?
- What can we leave out?
- What can we bypass?
- Can we separate it into different parts? How useful

is each of the parts? Could we improve it one part at a time?

– What isn't the problem?

Rearrange

When it comes down to it, creativity is really about rearranging what we know to form something we didn't know. You can rearrange letters or words to spark a new thought. For instance, instead of saying how can we sell more bottles, you might ask how can we bottle more sales. Does this make you look at the problem a little differently?

Can you rearrange the way you price a product or service in order to sell more? Xerox had a hard time when it first started selling copiers because the equipment was so expensive it often took a vote by the board of directors to make the sale happen. So, they decided to start putting copiers in place and charge per copy instead. So instead of capital expenditure for a copier, the copies became a petty cash expense.

So, as you are using the rearrangement approach to creativity, here are some questions to ask. How else can this subject be arranged? Is there an arrangement that would work better?

What other layout or pattern would work better?

Can you change the sequence? Can you change the timing, pace, or schedule?

Reverse

Let's reverse our perspective by asking "what is the opposite of this?" This is what Henry Ford did when he thought about how work was done. Instead of bringing people to the work, he wondered how it would affect the process if he brought the work to the people, and the assembly line was born. Ford's innovation brought the average Model-T Ford cost down to $350 from $950 in eight years.

So, as you are considering your problem, it is about transposing the positives and negatives. For instance, at one time incurring corporate debt was anathema. Henry Kravis didn't see it that way and he came up with the idea of the leveraged buyout as a means of buying control from stockholders.

Can you turn it around, or up instead of down?

Can relationships be reversed?

Imagine yourself as a member of the opposite sex. Does this change the way you approach the problem?

CHAPTER 8

A More Creative You

According to Nobel prize-winning chemist Linus Pauling, the best way to get a good idea is to get a lot of ideas. Unfortunately, school teaches us to find the right answer, when actually there is usually more than one right answer for a problem.

When an adult is challenged to come up ideas, he or she typically generates three to six possible solutions. The average child generates 60. We need to be more child-like in our approach to ideas. This is not to say that children are more creative. They just haven't been beaten down by naysayers yet. Your God-given innate creative abilities are limitless and don't let anyone convince you otherwise. You are creative.

I hope now that you have read this book, you will start thinking more like a child and looking for all the answers not just the ones society expects you to find. Once you begin doing this, you will free your mind, and a free mind will take you wherever you want to go. Happy travels, creative thinker.

Creativity Resources

BOOKS

How to Think Like Leonardo da Vinci – Great book by Michael Gelb that lays out da Vinci's approach to thinking.

Thinkertoys – In this revised and expanded edition of his groundbreaking *Thinkertoys*, creativity expert Michael Michalko reveals life-changing creativity tools that will help you think like a genius.

Creativity, Inc. – Ed Catmull's New York Times Bestseller is an incisive book about creativity in business.

ONLINE

Artist's Tool Kit – http://www.artsconnected.org/toolkit/explore.cfm – Artists use visual elements and principles like line, color and shape as tools to build works of art. This tool kit helps you explore these principles.

Big Dig – http://www.idea-sandbox.com/innovation-tools/bigdig/ – A sandbox full of thought-starters collected from great thinkers and writers. Click to dig up an idea. Don't like that suggestion? Dig again.

Bomomo – http://bomomo.com/ – An online drawing tool with a host of textures you can employ in your creations.

Bubbl.Us – https://bubbl.us/ – An elegant, easy-to-use mind-mapping tool. The free version gets you up to three mind maps.

Canva – https://www.canva.com/ – The online creation tool that is great for creating text and image content suitable for use on your blog, Instagram, Linkedin and other social media platforms.

Cloud Dreamer – http://invention.si.edu/cloud-dreamer – Pretend play helps us learn to think visually and spatially and to both capture and express ideas. Cloud Dreamer is all about pretending.

Coffivity – https://coffitivity.com/ – This website recreates the ambient sounds of a cafe to boost your creativity and help you work better.

Creative Think – http://creativethink.com/ – Creativity expert, Roger von Oech's, website contains a number of good creativity tools to enhance your thinking.

CreativeWritingPrompts.com – More than 300 writing prompts to get the little gray cells working.

Damn Interesting – http://www.damninteresting.com/ – A website that shares fascinating but obscure true stories from science, history, and psychology since 2005. Random fodder for the brain.

Diffen – http://www.diffen.com/ – One of these things is not like the other! Use Diffen to compare and contrast two things.

Do   Nothing   For   Two   Minutes   –
http://www.donothingfor2minutes.com/ – A website
that provides you with calming white noise, a nice
photo, and a clock that begins a two-minute countdown
once you have stopped doing any work on your
computer.

50 Tools Which Can Help You In Your Writing –
http://www.lifehack.org/articles/lifehack/fifty-50-tools-
which-can-help-you-in-writing.html – This is an old – but
still relevant – list of creativity tools to give your writing
a boost.

Afterword

Thanks so much for reading *Born Creative*. I hope you enjoyed it and can find a way to utilize your improved creativity to build a better life.

I thrive on feedback – so love it or hate it – please feel free to review the book. This helps make my next work stronger.

I have two other books out now: _Get Glad: A Practical Guide To A Happier Life_ and The Dad's Book Of Jokes.

If you read them, please let me know what you think by reviewing them.

About Harry Hoover

Harry is an author, content developer, creativity facilitator, and speaker. His communications career spans more than 35 years and runs the gamut from print and broadcast journalism, government, and corporate communications to advertising and public relations agencies. He has owned two advertising agencies and is now a freelance writer.

His other books include *Moving to Charlotte: The Un-Tourist Guide, Get Glad: Your Practical Guide To A Happier Life,* and *The Dad's Book Of Jokes.*

Follow Harry:

Facebook.com/uimproved

https://www.linkedin.com/in/harryhoover/

Printed in the USA
CPSIA information can be obtained
at www.ICGtesting.com
LVHW050209121223
766264LV00043B/762

9 780692 580905